Snug as a B...

Written and Illustrated
by Mal Peet and Elspeth Graham

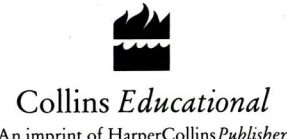

Collins *Educational*
An imprint of HarperCollins*Publishers*

Hanging beds, hairy beds, old beds, cold beds, posh beds, poor beds, soft beds and silly beds...

This is a book about all sorts of beds.

Stone-Age beds

Thousands of years ago, when people lived in caves or stone huts, beds were just heaps of straw and leaves on the ground. Furry animal skins were used for blankets.

The whole family shared one bed. And they shared it with spiders and fleas and all sorts of tickly, itchy, biting bugs, too.

*Good night, sleep tight,
Don't let the bedbugs bite.
If they do, grab a shoe
And beat them till they're
Black and blue.*

In bed in Ancient Egypt

Beds in Ancient Egypt were often decorated with painted carvings of animals. The head end of the bed was sometimes higher than the foot end, which meant sleeping on a slope.

The Ancient Egyptians used curved wooden headrests as pillows.

Would you like an extra pillow, dear?

Romans asleep at the table

In Ancient Rome, rich people often had meals which went on for hours.
They lay on big couches to eat.
Perhaps this was to save them the trouble of getting to bed when they were full up.

Asleep with the sheep

In the past, people who lived in cold countries shared their houses with their farm animals. In wintertime, the animals were brought inside.

Some families slept on a platform above the animals. It was smelly up there, but it was warm.

Hanging around in hammocks

Old sailing ships were too small and crowded for everyone to have a bunk. Sailors slept in **hammocks** which could be hung up almost anywhere.
In the daytime the hammocks were rolled up and put away.

Another good thing about hammocks was that when the ship rocked from side to side, the hammock didn't!

Hammocks had other uses too.

Sleeping on top of the stove

In freezing cold Siberia, the big wood-burning stove was the most important part of the house.

During the day it was used for cooking and heating water. At night, people slept on it, and beside it, and above it on big wooden shelves.

My bed is a box!

About 300 years ago many people lived in draughty stone cottages. One way of keeping warm at night was to sleep in a **box bed**. These beds were built inside a big cupboard near the fire.

My bed is a tent!

Some rich and powerful people lived in palaces, and slept in great big **four-poster beds**. Thick heavy curtains hung all around the bed to keep the draughts out.

Beds like these were very expensive.

I'm the boss so I'm staying in bed

Staying in bed was one way of showing how rich and powerful you were. About 350 years ago, the most powerful man in France was Cardinal Richelieu. He spent a lot of time in bed. He even travelled around in bed.

If the Cardinal visited a house where the door wasn't big enough for him and his bed to get through, his men would knock a hole in the wall.

Warming the bed

What warms *your* bed on chilly nights?
A snug electric blanket?
A nice soft hot-water bottle?
But what did people do before these things were invented?

Rich people sometimes made a servant get into their bed first to warm it up.

A warming pan, with hot coals inside, could be used instead.

A hot brick wrapped in a cloth was another way to warm the bed.

Hot-water bottles made of pottery were useful for warming the sheets.

But they often leaked.

Curved hot-water bottles were called 'belly warmers'.

Hot coals were put into this bed wagon and it was slipped in between the sheets.

And who was the brave person who tested the first electric blanket?

Hanging about in bed

Once upon a time, mothers hung their babies' cradles in trees, so that the wind would rock them gently to and fro.

Chinese and American-Indian mothers used the same trick.

Hush-a-bye baby, in the tree top.
When the wind blows, the cradle will rock.
When the bough breaks, the cradle will fall,
And down will come baby, cradle and all.

Who would sleep in these beds?

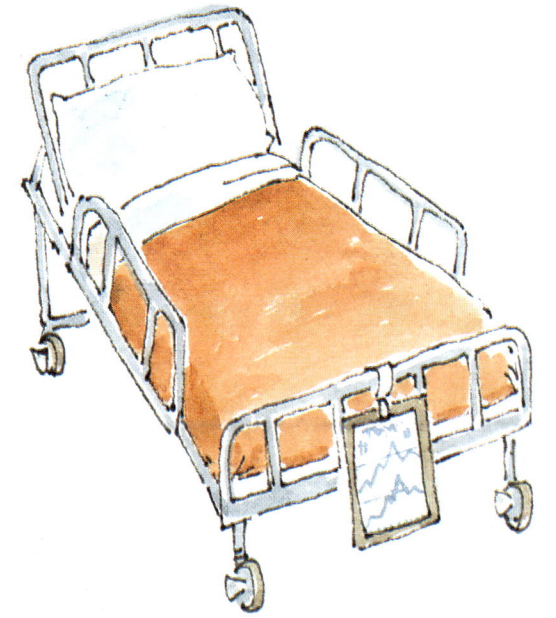

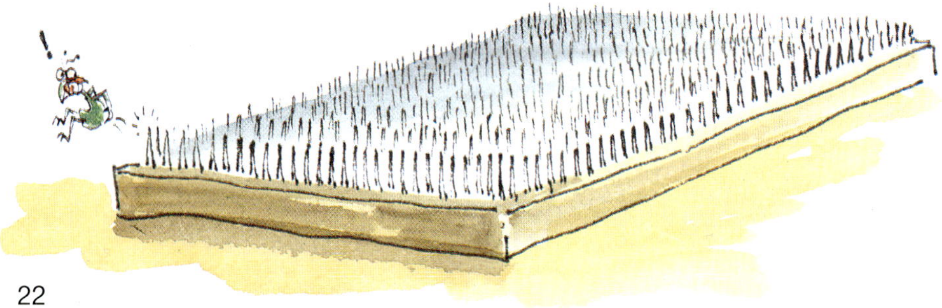